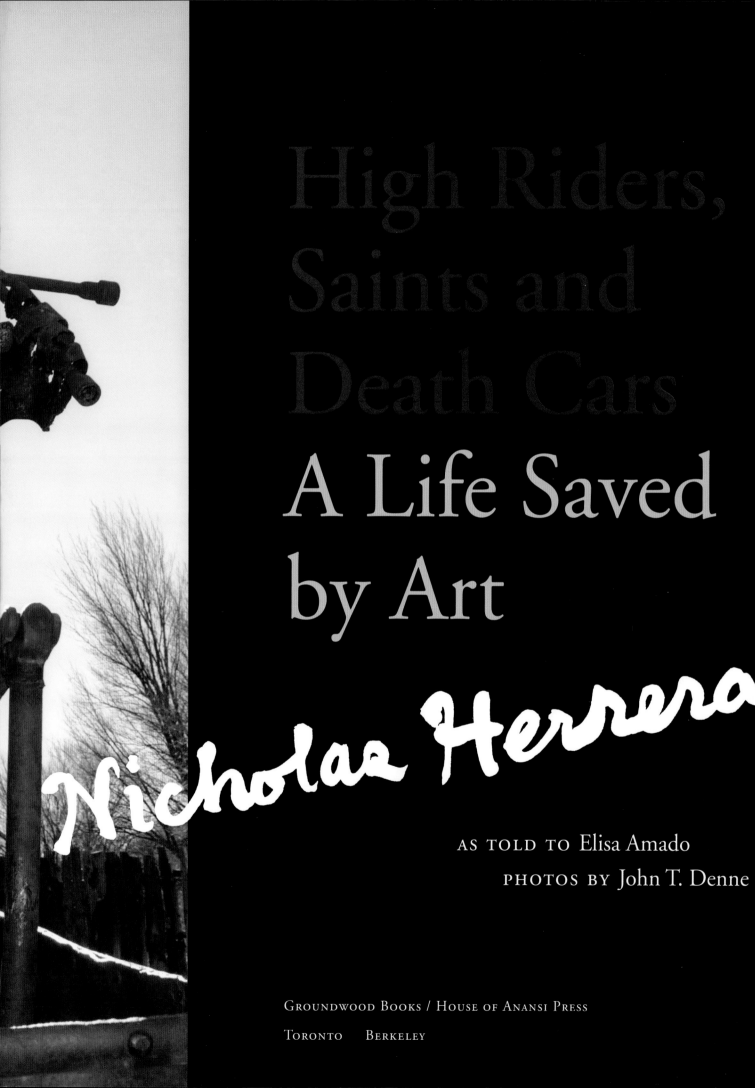

High Riders, Saints and Death Cars

A Life Saved by Art

Nicholas Herrera

AS TOLD TO Elisa Amado

PHOTOS BY John T. Denne

GROUNDWOOD BOOKS / HOUSE OF ANANSI PRESS

TORONTO   BERKELEY

**"Even when I was twelve I was already out
of control,"** says New Mexico folk artist Nicholas Herrera. His
mother wondered if he would survive his wild lifestyle. When he was in
his twenties he nearly died in a car accident because he had been drinking. But he lived, and went on to become a folk artist whose work is
sought after by museums and private collectors. As Nicholas says, his life
was saved by art — *"El arte me salvó la vida."* This is his story.

Nicholas lives in the town of El Rito. His family has occupied the same
land for about two hundred years. He sleeps and eats in one house, makes
his art in another — his studio — and shows his art in yet another. He
works as a welder and mechanic on old cars in another house and keeps
his chickens in the oldest structure — a *jacal*, or kind of shed — where his
grandparents and great-grandparents once lived. He shares this land with
his daughter, who visits him every weekend, and with his mother, whom
he buried in a building beside the house in which he grew up.

The chapel of St. Anthony, where Nicholas tends the shrine to his mother, Celia.

"My mother said, 'I don't want to be buried in the cemetery,'" Nicholas explains. "And when she got sick she told me she wanted to be here. So I started digging, but she said, 'Take me into the house. I'm not dead yet.'

"When she died I made her a chapel. It's dedicated to St. Anthony. She was the president of the St. Anthony Society for years. He's the saint you pray to when you lose things."

El Rito Fire. In this painting of the ranch, angels help to soak the dry land. A major fire in 2006 burned large areas of the surrounding mountains. Nicholas, a volunteer firefighter, works to control the blaze.

A view of El Rito's main street, with the mountains in the background.

The Herrera land lies in a valley. Up beyond the hills is the *potrero* (horse meadow), which was deeded to his family in the early 1820s. As Nicholas says, "It's pretty amazing that I can be down here where my great-grandfather was and up there in the *potrero* where he was, too."

Nicholas's family first arrived in the New World with the Spanish conquistadors in the early 1500s. They came from the Canary Islands and from Estremadura province, one of the poorest and most barren in Spain —a fact that has been blamed for the hardness and cruelty of many of the conquistadors.

As Nicholas says, "The conquistadors wanted to kick ass. Those conquistadors were a trip. We, the Herreras, have that blood. That's why I don't drink. I get mean. When I drink, the conquistador in me comes out. Crazy stuff."

His ancestors rode up from Mexico with Juan de Oñate in 1598. Oñate was the man who first brought Spanish domination to what is now New Mexico, conquering the Pueblo Indians in the process. The Pueblos fought back and threw the Spaniards out of New Mexico in the Pueblo Revolt of 1680.

The Herrera family had to move to Texas, but they returned after twelve years and have been in this very beautiful part of the world ever since. There was intermarriage between the Native Americans, who occupied the land originally, and the descendants of the Spaniards. Despite that, relations between the two groups are still not easy. Nicholas says, "The Indians want to make us feel guilty. But we taught them how to use metal and brought sheep and horses."

Over the centuries, the Herrera family were farmers and merchants and soldiers who fought for the US in World War I and World War II. But they were also artists. For many generations men in the Herrera family have been members of a group called the Penitentes — devout Catholics who join together to pray for people who have died. The saints of the Church are very important to them. Nicholas's great-uncle, José Inés Herrera, was a Penitente and a well-known santero — an artist who makes representations of saints. He was known as *"El Santero de la Muerte,"* or the man who makes images of death. But there was no market for his art in those days — it was made for religious purposes.

Nicholas's mother, Celia, also made art all her life. She drew scenes of the farm and household with crayon and paper, and even carved some saints. She couldn't do this often, as she had three very active sons. But as she grew older, she had more time to make images. In 1998 there was a gallery show of her pictures.

Despite all the artists in the family, no one but his mother could have guessed that Nicholas would become such an important creator of political and religious art in the santero tradition. When he was twelve, he carved a sculpture of Roberta Brosseau — a woman his mother worked for. It's called *Lady with Diamond Eyes*, because Nick thought her eyes were very beautiful.

Artwork by Celia Herrera.

Lady with Diamond Eyes. Nick's portrait of Roberta Brosseau, who was a friend of the painter Georgia O'Keeffe.

Rubel Herrera, 1915. Nicholas's grandfather and nephew of José Inés Herrera, he served in France in World War I.

Nicholas's dad, Pedro Herrera, in his army uniform, 1944.

Death Cart,
1890-1910,
José Inés Herrera.
This typical death
cart sculpture is
made of pine and
carved cottonwood,
gesso, paint, feather,
silk and hair.

Of all the people in Nicholas's young life, his mother was probably the most important: "My mom was very nice. She knew how to deal with me real good. She'd gather the kids that I made trouble with and make *sopapillas* and then take us out into the wood to look for sticks and stones and things and then everything would be fine."

School was another story. When Nick was in second grade, a teacher asked him and his two best friends what they wanted to be. "A bank robber," was Nick's reply. "A pimp. A sheep herder," answered his friends. A later episode with the same teacher, which resulted in the death of her goldfish, ended in Nick and his friends being sent to "special ed."

He continued to struggle. It didn't help that Spanish was not taught in school, even though it was the language most of the kids spoke at home: "We weren't allowed to talk Spanish in school but we did anyway."

On top of that, Nick was dyslexic, though no one seemed to figure out why he was having trouble with reading. He and his friends were simply passed up the ladder year after year. They were scratched, slapped and mistreated, and any learning Nick did in this period was done on his own. "You just got to do it," he says.

Nicholas (far left) with his dad, mom and siblings at Christmas.

A crayon drawing by Celia. When she was old and had Alzheimer's, Celia did a lot of drawings like this. She liked to draw flowers and the thorns from Christ's crown as well as figures looking down from beyond.

Brothers Pete, Nicholas (center) and Ruben with their mother, Celia.

Nicholas (front center) with his older cousin Reg and his young family.

Nick, age five, with one of his pet goats. Chickens, ducks and dogs were also kept as pets by the children.

Celia (left) with her mother, Perfecta, and her sister, Valentina.

In the sixties, hippies came to town. "They were the first Anglos we had seen," says Nicholas. "We used to beg my parents to drive us in from the farm to the main street so we could watch the hippies walking around in their crazy clothes in front of Martin's Store." As Nick tells it, even the actor Dennis Hopper showed up, at the height of his fame as a biker in the movie *Easy Rider*.

For Nick, these hippie-sighting expeditions were as good as going to the movies. On the Fourth of July the town would be treated to a Hippie Parade. And Nick and his teenaged friends would sneak down to the river to watch the hippie girls swimming nude.

Many of the Spanish and Indian men of El Rito had fought in World War II and in Korea, and a number were currently fighting in Vietnam. They didn't appreciate the hippies, or the fact that they may have been draft dodgers or deserters. Nor did the community appreciate the drugs they brought in (Nick began smoking marijuana when he was thirteen). There were violent confrontations between the two groups, some involving shootings.

But hippies, drinking and drugs weren't the only kind of fun. Nicholas and his cousins formed a club called the Daredevils. They would place a bullet on a rock and stand around in a circle throwing rocks at it until it exploded. The person who made the bullet go off became a daredevil. Only cousins were allowed to join in this game, called "Playing Chicken," until a white boy proved that he was worthy by climbing out on a very thin branch to get a bird's nest.

Nicholas grew into a handsome young teenager who would dress up "just like John Travolta" to dance salsa and rock and roll in town. And he had many girlfriends. "If a girl had a house and a car, I was there — party time!" he laughs. His other friends were also wild, and the fun and games were irresistible.

Nick at fifteen.

Nicholas Prays for a Santo Chevy, self-portrait. This sculpture shows Nicholas praying for a 1939 Chevy painted in a 1960s hot rod flame motif. His prayer was answered!

Yet at the same time that he was living the wild life, Nicholas became a Penitente like his father, grandfather and uncles before him. He was constantly torn between the crazy sex, drugs and rock-and-roll lifestyle on the one hand and renouncing all this to be an upstanding citizen. "The devil's always there," he smiles. "You are fighting the demons — you feel guilty — but then you have another drink and you feel better."

"They let me get out of high school in eleventh grade," Nicholas remembers. "I took a welding class at community college and I loved it. I got certified in six months. It usually takes a year and a half. Hanging out with old guys. I took auto body for custom cars. But I never wanted a diploma. I just wanted to be able to do it."

He tried to join the army, but he couldn't because of his dyslexia: "I wanted to be a marine like my brother. I would have come out worse than I was. I wanted to kill. I was full of energy. It was crazy. You don't know how to use it. Later I put it in my art."

Your Choice — Heaven and Hell. This work shows children watching helplessly as their parents are tempted by the devil with drugs and alcohol. The devil's shirt is inscribed "DOC" as a joke, because what he offers makes you feel good, but ultimately destroys you. Christ stands next to the devil with a warning gesture. The piece shows two roads — *El camino de Dios*, with a sign reading "Heaven 500 Miles," and *El camino del diablo*, with

a sign reading "Hell 2 Miles." In another view of the work we can see that the road to heaven is "*Santa Fe y Familia*," or Faith and Family, and the road to hell is a "Dead End." Nicholas says this is among his most powerful pieces.

Since Nicholas couldn't be a soldier, he became a fireman, fighting fires all over the West. He also got a construction job at Los Alamos — the place where the first atomic bomb was made, and still a major center for the nuclear weapons industry. His dad had worked at Los Alamos in the fifties because it was impossible to support his family as a farmer.

Despite having jobs that made him some money, Nicholas continued to be torn between his crazy life and his growing interest in art, and the inner knowledge that his actions were dangerous and destructive. Much of his later art shows this struggle between the good life and the bad.

Mi vida de 25 (My Life at 25). One of the sculpted works depicting Nicholas's car accident.

Walking the Line. In this work Nicholas, suspected of drunk driving, has been stopped by the police. The officer is asking him to walk in a straight line to test him. The "E" on the mountain in the background can also be seen in the photo of El Rito on page 7. It was made by local high school students to represent the Eagles, their sports team.

Mi vida de 25 (My Life at 25). Another work with this title shows Nicholas lying in a coma in hospital.

His mother said, "If he makes it to twenty-five he'll make it." But there were times when it didn't seem like he would.

Nicholas had begun to finance his wild ways with art. He'd make a *retablo* (wooden painting of a saint), sell it and then use the money to go back to drinking and driving. Slowly the making of art was becoming more and more interesting to him. But this didn't stop him from driving a car one day while he was drunk.

He had a head-on crash with a truck. The car flipped over and Nicholas was thrown to the side of the road. He says he could see what was happening, including himself lying by the road, as the ambulance and cops came: "I remember seeing the car, the wreck. I came out of my own body. And I could hear Ritchie Valens singing 'La Bamba' on the car radio."

He remained in a coma for weeks. His friend brought *retablos* that Nicholas had made and propped them up around his bed. At first the doctors told his mother he would probably die, but suddenly there was a turn for the better and he began to wake up.

After he recovered, Nicholas had to serve some time in jail for having driven while he was drunk. But he has not had a drink or used drugs since that day. He turned his back on his crazy friends. "I had to," he says. And he began to make art the center of his life: "That's what it took for me to change, imagine. It's horrible to grow up like that when addiction takes over. After that accident I felt different. I was done with it. It's like something came out of me. I was reborn."

His old friends would come by, but they soon realized that he had changed, and they didn't want to be with him unless he would join them in drinking. A lot of those people have since died.

Los Alamos Death Truck.
Nicholas's father, who worked as a janitor in the Los Alamos National Laboratory machine shop, died of radiation poisoning.

Los Alamos Death Truck, detail. Nicholas named the driver and crew, who appear as skeletons, Vato, Loco and Man (Dude, Crazy and Man). The sculpture pays homage to "the workers who do the dirty work at Los Alamos."

Nicholas turned to making art in a serious way when he lost his job at Los Alamos. For one thing, he realized that his work was dangerous, that workers risked getting radiation sickness. When he was asked to clean up some radioactive waste, he said to the supervisor, "I'll do it, but only if your kid works with me." And that was the end of his time at Los Alamos.

He has made many sculptures on this theme — each called *Los Alamos Death Truck* — which show trucks carrying radioactive material away from the plant. (Sometimes he includes a death figure smoking dope, sitting on the barrels of waste.)

"I decided that I didn't want to waste my time," Nicholas says. "I didn't know if I would make it as an artist. But that's what I wanted to be. I started going around to museums and galleries, looking around, asking questions. The art world was surprised to see someone as young as me who was so ambitious. So they helped me."

Protect and Serve.

happens in town, you get blamed — but you're innocent.

That's why I had Jesus in the cop car.

"I did some crazy pieces, for example, this Jesus in the back of a cop car, which I made when I was twenty-five.

"When you're young and have a bad reputation, everything bad that happens in town, you get blamed—but you're innocent. That's why I had Jesus in the cop car. If Jesus came into the world now, that's what they'd do with him. People don't like the real deal. That's what art is all about."

This work is now in the Smithsonian Institution, one of the foremost museums in the United States. It was sold to the museum by the Rosenak family, who were the first major collectors to buy Nicholas's work. They found Nick at the Santa Fe Spanish Market, where the Spanish community shows art and crafts. Artists sit in their booths and chat with possible buyers. When the Rosenaks heard Nicholas's story, they realized he was for real and became serious collectors of his work. At one time they owned almost thirty pieces. Their collection helped to make Nicholas known. They opened doors for him. After that he met more and more people. He explains that that's how things work in the art world.

Nicholas assembling motorcycle-themed sculptures using found materials, and welding.

Even though Nicholas works in the santero tradition, he really is different from other santeros. For one thing, he uses a huge amount of recycled material.

When he was a kid he found a rich friend's bike abandoned by the side of the road. He took it home, added high handlebars, a souped-up seat and painted it crazy colors. This was really his first high rider. Its former owner didn't even recognize it by the time Nick was through with it and praised him for his "cool" bike. It showed Nick that he could make something out of whatever was lying around — old cars, collapsed houses and things left by the side of the road: "It's always been recycling for me. Stuff I find. I get beams from old houses. That's my material because it has history. It's always been important to me — the history."

Nick's art supplies!

The work **Biker por Vida** is seen in this photograph (above) taken just before the funeral procession of Nicholas's friend Armando Trujillo.

Giving up drink and drugs did not mean that Nicholas became tame and boring or even that he began to live safely. Cars and motorcycles are ongoing themes in his art, as well as in his day-to-day life.

One of Nicholas's best friends, Armando Trujillo, was killed in a motorcycle accident in 1994. The sculpture Nick made to commemorate his friend's life — *Biker por Vida* (*Biker for Life*) — was created in part with materials that came from the bike his friend was riding when he had the accident.

"We used to ride our bikes together," Nicholas remembers. "But he had an accident. He was run over. He lived for a while, then he died. I used a lot of parts — the pipes, the emblems and stuff like that from the bike he died on — to make this piece."

He also made a small wooden sculpture of his friend as a *muerte* (an image of death) for the Day of the Dead. These works were displayed at a celebration of Armando's life held at the Museum of International Folk Art in Santa Fe. A procession of about fifty bikers and low-rider cars drove to the museum to unveil the pieces. It was hardly a typical art-world opening, with a noisy procession of dozens of bikers and low riders winding its way to the party. This unusual and groundbreaking event was named *Cruzando Fronteras* (Crossing Borders).

The reason I have them on a trike **is that the Holy Family**

is going through a dangerous time...

Even today Nicholas continues to explore the theme of bikes and danger. This extraordinary piece, *The Three Kings*, tells the story of the Nativity, with the Holy Family riding a V8 trike accompanied by the Three Kings on motorcycles. V8 trikes are built using the V8 engines from cars. The engines are mounted on tubes to create a trike that can go dangerously fast.

The Three Kings. Nicholas's elaborate retelling of the Holy Family's flight into Egypt. In the left niche St. Michael defeats the devil to prevent him from using his cell phone to tip off Herod's thugs (the police).

The Three Kings, detail. In the central niche one king holds the baby Jesus and another bears a low-rider toy.

The Three Kings, detail. The Holy Family on their V8 trike, followed by the kings.

"The reason I have them on a trike is that the Holy Family is going through a dangerous time at that moment," Nicholas explains. When the Three Kings told King Herod that they had seen a miraculous baby in a stable, the king put out a death warrant for all newborn baby boys to make sure that this special one would not grow up to be his rival. The Holy Family fled to Egypt to escape this massacre.

This piece is an example of how Nicholas combines his own interests and the modern world with stories from the Bible to create very powerful sculptures.

Nicholas with "La Bomba." He holds a portrait of the car in a desert landscape.

La Bomba. The painting emphasizes the car's use as a commercial vehicle. The lettering on the door reads "El Santero del Rito."

Nicholas rebuilt "La Bomba" shortly after he came out of jail. It kept him busy and away from doing "bad stuff." Even as a young artist he was combining religious images and vehicles. He found the car junked in an *arroyo* (dry riverbed). He saved it, painted it and then drove it in the procession to the museum for the commemoration of Armando Trujillo's life.

Nicholas isn't really interested in cars for themselves, but because of how they look. Pieces of cars are often incorporated into his art. Cars are mythic objects from the wild teen culture that he embraced as a young man. Combining the sacred with the profane, such as painting Jesus on a car with flames and spider webs, happens all the time in his art.

Low Rider Wedding. Nicholas does not see these *muertes* as frightening. Instead they show "Marriage 'til death do us part." The use of customized low-rider cars for the bride and groom in wedding parties is common in northern New Mexico.

"Cars don't go away for me," Nicholas says. "I think I'm not interested in them anymore, then all of a sudden I find myself doing some. I like vintage cars. I like how they were designed. They were class. I can make great things from them. I find them in junkyards and *arroyos*. I bring them back to life."

21st Century Executive Cruiser.
Nicholas works to turn the front
of a bus into a beautiful and
useful desk. The original 1940
bus was used to chauffeur the
nuns from the convent in El Rito
as they went about their duties.
The finished desk (top right)
is now in Nicholas's sculpture
studio and is used to this day.

This car is called "The Babemobile," and the back
seat is red velvet. For years Nicholas would drive it up to
Taos, where there are many art galleries. As he became
better known as an artist, women flocked to him, attract-
ed by his talent and charm.

But they're disappointed by life in El Rito, he says:
"I've had girlfriends who are all romantic and think it
will be fun to live here but they don't last. Maybe they
got their idea of the country from the show 'Little House
on the Prairie.' After being here for three weeks they can't
stand it and they leave."

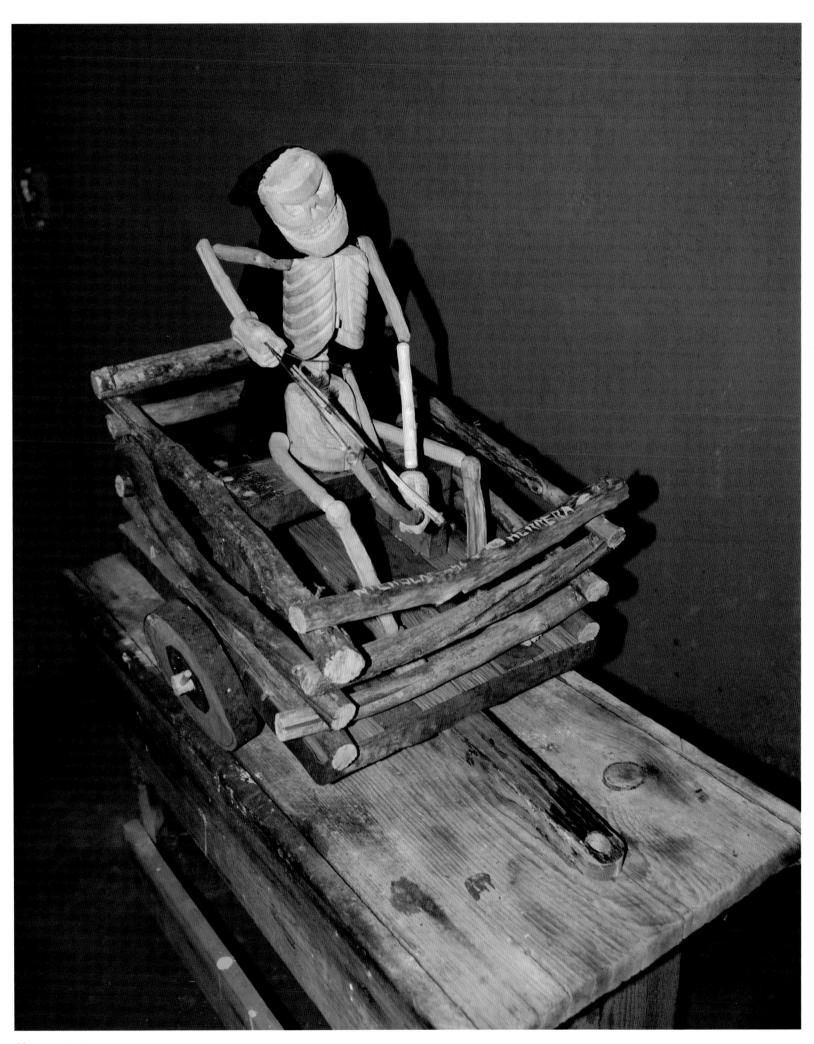

A death cart with an archer *muerte* is like the *muertes* that Nicholas's great-uncle used to make.

A death cart with a drunken rider. He plays a guitar and keeps a "Bud kegger" handy.

Death carts are carvings of skeletons riding in carts. They are a very old form of religious art that comes from the Penitente tradition in New Mexico. Nicholas has made death carts all his life as an artist, but always with his own twist.

"The first time I saw a death cart I was at a *morada* when I was twelve," he says. "They told me that the santero who made this was my uncle. I put two and two together. I figured out, no wonder I love to make things so much. It's in my blood. I carved a little *muerte* of my own right away.

"At a *morada* the Penitentes carry the death carts outside and take them for a walk all around, so that we remember that we are all going to die some day. It's part of who we are. We're all going to die. I take the same idea, the *muerte*, and make it modern with a motorcycle or a gun or a syringe— modern death. I do them my own way. They are scary but they are my friends. I'm still a Penitente. I still go and pray."

And he still makes death carts.

As Nicholas became better known as an artist, another major event took place in his life — the birth of his daughter, Elena: "My child — Elena Sybella Clark Backus y Herrera — is the daughter of Susan Backus, who had the Big Sun Gallery in Taos. We started dating. I was visiting Seville, in Spain, and I found myself kneeling in the cathedral praying for a baby. A month later Susan told me she was pregnant. At first I was scared. You freak out. I'm not used to doing this.

"Then everything changes. All of a sudden it comes naturally. Before that everything was about me. After that — no more. You have to face your responsibilities. I sold my motorcycle when my daughter was born. How can you have a motorcycle and a kid? I'd already lived the party-life stuff. I don't miss it. Her mom and I are good friends."

Elena, age three (left), and at nine.

"My mother had bad Alzheimer's when Susan was pregnant, but she would remember and whisper "Baby, baby" every time she saw her. And luckily she was still alive when Elena was born."

Elena, who is now eleven, spends the weekends with Nicholas, and she makes art, too. "Elena's a little artist," says her father. "She has commissions already. She sold twenty-four pieces at a recent studio tour. Twenty to thirty bucks for each piece. She has to start at the bottom. You have to get on the ladder. You can't get on the elevator. In school they aren't so interested in art. And they don't teach her Spanish. I speak it to her but she isn't into it."

Nicholas also makes Elena take walks, even if she doesn't feel like it. He's quite a strict parent. "You've got to work with kids," he says. "You've got to be ahead of their game. But they are so much fun when they're little.

"It's hard to bring a child into this world. Everything is so commercial. They think you have to give them everything. They don't want to work. We had nothing when I was a kid. We always made all our toys. Every car I owned I bought myself and fixed it with parts from other cars."

Nicholas remains very much a part of the santero tradition. These pieces, called *retablos* when they are painted on wood or *bultos* when they are sculptures, show saints with their attributes — for example, the bird for St. Francis, the sword and scales for St. Michael, the plow for St. Isidore the farmer.

Nicholas has read many books about the saints. He looks for inspiration in movies and in the Bible, especially the Old Testament. But his interest lies in taking these traditional themes and making them into relevant contemporary pieces — to turn the artistic tradition in a different direction: "I'm part of the tradition but I'm different. I use it and make it into my own. That's what's cool about it."

Jesus and the Trinity

San Isidro (St. Isidore). Nicholas's many images of the patron saint of farmers also include depictions of the saint riding a tractor.

An array of Nick's santos (saints), in painting and sculpture. *Clockwise from top left:*

St. Francis of Assisi

Crucifixion

Christ showing his wounds to St. Thomas.

Joan of Arc

Our Lady of Guadalupe. This collaborative piece features tinwork by Nicholas's friend J.D. Martinez.

San Juan Nepomuceno, the patron saint of El Rito and the Penitentes

St. Gertrude

St. Francis of Assisi

St. Michael

St. Michael. This panel is done in sgraffito. The white lines are rapidly scratched with a nail into wet black paint.

Crucifixion with angels

Pope John Paul II

Like everybody, Nicholas has to make a living. He started selling his art in the Santa Fe Spanish Market where the Rosenaks discovered him. But he wasn't crazy about sitting in a booth all day making small talk. Also, his work didn't really fit into the kind of traditional folk art being sold in that market, or even into the general New Mexican folk art tradition. As more people collected his work, he began to show it in folk art galleries.

"Some collectors are like family to me. But some don't want to meet the artist. I've dealt with a lot of people in the world. I don't have any education but I'm smart about things like that. A lot of people like me because I'm real. They like me or they don't.

"When I started," he says, "folk art wasn't very valuable. People buy art at the market because they think they can get a better deal. Now I've moved to fine art galleries. Prices in art galleries are higher. And I'm showing with all kinds of different artists. Galleries get 50 to 60 percent of the price. I get the rest. But I don't mind because they have a lot of expenses."

The Spanish Market depicted in a sculpture of that name.

The Spanish Market in Santa Fe.

A gallery in Nicholas's studio. Every October
the artists in El Rito participate in open houses,
the El Rito Studio Tour.

Are the wars really about liberating anyone?

Or are they about money?

And who is paying the price?

Young collectors are also interested in Nicholas's work. Curt Nonomaque is in his forties. He owns several pieces. "Curt—he likes the theme of my art, the history of it," says Nicholas. "A lot of artists are having trouble now, but I seem to be doing okay. Because I've got work in museums I seem to have a good track record."

One reason for Nicholas's ongoing success may be his intense involvement with the modern world—what it's like and how it's changing—and with the political issues that interest him. *Let's Party (Desert Storm)*, for example, was made in response to the Gulf War. Nicholas says, "Once the war started, when you would open up the TV that was all you saw. You couldn't think about anything else. I thought to myself, I might as well do something about it."

One thing that disturbs Nicholas is that the people who go to war and do the fighting are people like him. It's not the kids of politicians and rich people who are placed in danger. "Poor people go because they need a check. So if we have to go to war, then let's get it over with," says Nicholas. "Are the wars really about liberating anyone? Or are they about money? And who is paying the price?"

Let's Party (Desert Storm).

Liberty.

An Uncle Sam *muerte*.

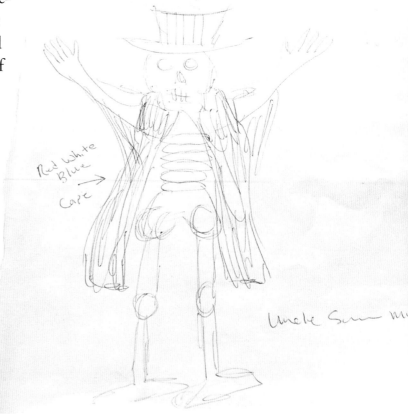

Red White Blue → Cape

Uncle Sam mu

He was also deeply affected by 9/11. A month before the planes hit the towers Nicholas had lunch at the top of one of the buildings in a restaurant called Windows on the World. He remembers the faces of the people that he saw there, especially the serving staff, and wonders, "Did they live or die?"

He made a number of pieces about the towers. At around the same time, he made other political pieces, such as this drawing of Uncle Sam. "Uncle Sam will take your money if you don't watch out," he laughs.

He has made a Statue of Liberty dressed as Adelita — the Mexican revolutionary — carrying a rifle and wearing a bandolier filled with bullets. Adelita is a symbol of oppressed people taking power into their own hands and rising up against the rich. Throughout his career as an artist, Nicholas has sided with the poor.

Jesus and the Twin Towers.

Santa Barbara Bless New York. St. Barbara is the patron saint of firefighters. The words at the base of the statue read, "In memory of New York fire fighters police and all people who died Sept 11th."

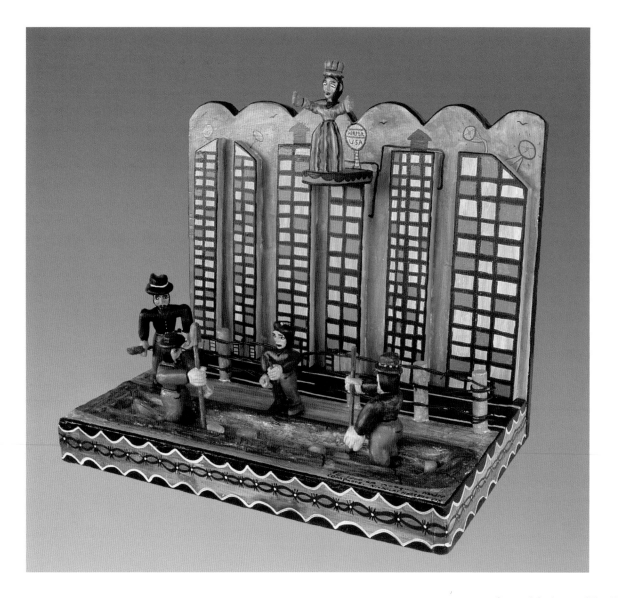

Se acabó el agua (The Water Is Gone). This work deals with the huge "thirst" of big cities and the lack of water on the surrounding lands.

The things that are happening close to home are very important to Nicholas right now. Some of his most significant political pieces have been created around the idea that land and water should not be sold — *La Tierra y el Agua no se Venden*. They refer to what might be called the gentrification of the US Southwest.

Nicholas explains, "There's never been much water here. Then an agreement was made to send water to Texas. So we have hardly any water left. It's a big problem. Water is very important, and rich people in Albuquerque and Santa Fe are drilling wells and emptying the aquifer. Politicians are letting it happen."

According to Nicholas, other major users of water are the Native American-owned casinos. They use the water for their gambling establishments and golf courses: "I think the Spanish should stop going to the casinos. We are the biggest users of the casinos and the biggest losers when it comes to water rights."

The Land Is Not for Sale. In the framed panel is a typical idyllic scene of a ranch. The sculptures in the foreground show Nicholas and a friend saying "No!" to a lawyer carrying a briefcase stuffed with cash. Above the grill of the lawyer's car Nicholas has inscribed "BMW."

Night Riders, detail.

As for the land, "People with big bucks are buying it up. Every time a gringo buys land it gets more expensive. A two-million-dollar home is built next to a fifty-thousand-dollar home. Spanish people can't afford to buy these houses anymore. So they have to go into low-income housing or a trailer court."

Conflict over who owns and gets to use land and water is part of New Mexican history. Nicholas's great-uncles joined a group called La Mano Negra, shown in the sculpture *Night Riders*. They rose up violently against a massive land grab by monied interests that began in the late 1800s, and eventually they were sent to jail and lost their land. As Nicholas says, "They were rebelling and they let it go to their heads."

To be a good artist, you need to work at it full-time. That means you have to make a living, and if you're a father, like Nick, support not only yourself but your child, too. Artists don't have salaries. They live off the sales of their art, one piece at a time, one customer at a time. So they have to be smart about how to sell their work.

Museums acquire art in different ways. Sometimes collectors sell their collections to them. Or a museum may want to buy a specific piece, so it must either find a patron who is willing to buy the piece and donate it, or get money from the state or local government. Sometimes the artist donates a piece. Nicholas does this—but only if he gets something in return. As he says, all his life he has lived in a kind of barter system, where you trade something for something else.

Having his art in museums makes Nicholas better known, which means he can sell his art for more money: "Now that I'm in museums I am getting more famous. The big pieces can sell for around ten to twenty thousand. I guess some people think they can make some money on me one of these days. I won an award from the Folk Art Society of America. I will be a featured artist at a big folk art convention coming up."

Making a living as an artist is never easy, even when you have a big reputation. In the past Nicholas made a lot of very big pieces. Now he's making smaller ones, because with the financial crisis the big pieces are getting harder to sell. It's not as easy for museums to find patrons.

But Nick just takes things in stride: "I have done really well at making a living. It's about how much you spend, too. If you live up here you don't need much. It's like being a farmer—there are lean years and rich years. I'm content with what I have. The more you have the more you want."

Brochures and flyers from Nicholas's many exhibitions over the years. After a period of success in New York, Nicholas was able to pay off his debts and buy the family land from his siblings. He says he never forgets how glad he is of that in lean times!

He believes that when someone buys his art they do it because they are getting something of long-term value. He knows collectors who sold off their art to get money to invest in the stock market, and then lost it all. He himself owns a lot of art by artist friends of his. It is good art, and over the years it will be worth a lot of money.

Young artists looking for a role model appreciate Nicholas's originality and are inspired by his success. As he says, "Lots of artists went to art school and all of a sudden they are copying my work."

Today he often works with young people: "What's really cool is I work with a lot of kids. They need a guide, encouragement. Most of the time they are quite talented. But they have to really get into it, like me. My mom guided me. She was there but I had to decide. If they don't get serious they won't become artists.

"Kids need art. The schools here spend so much money on sports. They build big stadiums for football. But if kids can play music or make any kind of art they could do so much more with their lives. Like me. That's why I work with them."

Nick's godson, Jerome (top); niece Leona (far left); and nephews Vincent and Urban (below).

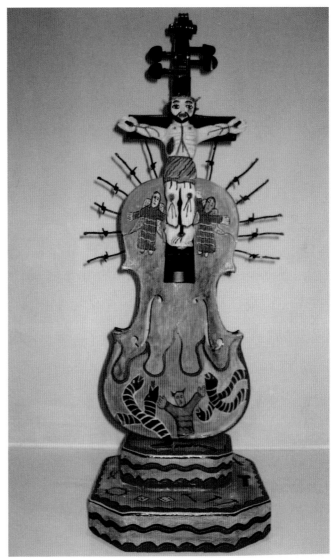

Nicholas donated this violin sculpture to a charity auction organized by the Santa Fe Symphony to buy musical instruments for children who cannot afford them. It fetched $8,000.

A great example of Nicholas's recent work is *La Percha de la Familia (The Family Clothesline)*.

Nicholas explains, "Everywhere I go there's a *percha*. It's something everyone looks at every day. When you see a *percha* in New Mexico, you know Spanish people live there.

"So I made this piece. The clothes are cut out from cars of the thirties, forties and fifties. The pants were a Cadillac, for example. They are in the original colors. And they have bullet holes in them because I found the cars in the *arroyos*, where they are used for target practice. The brassieres are headlights. My daughter designed some of the dresses. It was a fun piece to work on. I like making nice big pieces." He laughs, "Some people who live in a rich neighborhood are interested in buying it. But in those neighborhoods they aren't supposed to have clotheslines. How can they have it up in their yard, then?"

La Percha de la Familia,
detail and partial overview of
this outdoor sculpture.

El arte me salvó la vida.
(Art saved my life.)

Nicholas has lived through a lot. He almost died. He has lost his parents and many of his friends. He has had many girlfriends. He has a daughter and is a very good father. He has kept and taken care of the land that his ancestors owned and worked. And he has not only managed to make a living as an artist, he is recognized as one of the most interesting and original artists in New Mexico — one who has transcended the santero tradition and transformed it into fine art that speaks to many of the important issues of our times.

The Wheel of Life. A motorcycle tire and wheel support carry little scenes from Nicholas's life (clockwise from top): Nicholas as a newborn baby with his mother and father; as a child with toys he made himself; writing lines because of trouble at school; between his arguing parents; being punished at school; taking part in a procession of Penitentes; being tempted by the devil; "Jack Daniels" (the temptation of drink); being escorted to jail; the car accident; showing his art; and with Elena and family. The gold spiral spokes are derived from New Mexican decorative folk art. The fender is from a Harley-Davidson. In the hub is the Dove of Peace.

The Wheel of Life, detail: "Jack Daniels."

Nicholas works every day — on his art, on his houses and on being a father. He likes to be alone and go for long walks. And he is now in a good relationship with a woman.

As for what's next?

"I've got lots of sketchbooks full of ideas I haven't made. I'll make metal and wood pieces. I'm kind of interested in the contemporary part of art. I'll probably make less of the old traditional stuff."

He laughs his huge laugh.

"I'm going to keep doing my art. Until I'm dead, probably."

Unpainted figures from a
work in progress. The final
sculpture will depict Christ
escorted by two cops.

On the title page:
Muerte. A recent death cart
in which the figure is made
almost entirely of car parts.

Groundwood Books / House of Anansi Press
110 Spadina Avenue, Suite 801, Toronto, Ontario M5V 2K4
or c/o Publishers Group West
1700 Fourth Street, Berkeley, CA 94710

We acknowledge for their financial support of our publishing program the
Canada Council for the Arts, the Government of Canada through the Canada
Book Fund (CBF) and the Ontario Arts Council.

 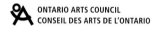

Canada Council   Conseil des Arts   ONTARIO ARTS COUNCIL
for the Arts   du Canada   CONSEIL DES ARTS DE L'ONTARIO

Library and Archives Canada Cataloguing in Publication
Herrera, Nicholas
High riders, saints and death cars : a life saved by art / Nicholas
Herrera ; as told to Elisa Amado.

ISBN 978-0-88899-854-5

1. Herrera, Nicholas — Juvenile literature.
2. Santos (Art) — New Mexico — Juvenile literature.
3. Santeros — New Mexico — Biography — Juvenile
literature. 4. Folk artists — United States — Biography —
Juvenile literature. I. Amado, Elisa II. Title.

N6537.H475A2 2011   j709.2   C2010-905905-0

Design by Michael Solomon
Printed and bound in China

PHOTO CREDITS
All photos are by John T. Denne with the exception of the
following:
8 (bottom), 10 (top), 11, 12, 17 (bottom), 24, 30, 31
(bottom), 34, 49 (top left and right): Courtesy of Nicholas
Herrera
9: Denver Art Museum Collection: general acquisition funds,
1948.22 © Denver Art Museum
13, 36, 37, 42 (top), 44, 45: Manitou Galleries, Santa Fe
14, 15: John Guernsey / Manitou Galleries, Santa Fe
16: Slotin Folk Art Auction
17 (top): Collection of the Haggerty Museum of Art,
Marquette University, Milwaukee, Wisconsin. Gift of Janice
and Chuck Rosenak
20: Smithsonian American Art Museum, Gift of Chuck and
Jan Rosenak and museum purchase through the Luisita L.
and Franz H. Denghausen Endowment
26, 27, 52, 53: David Michael Kennedy / Collection of
Curt Nonomaque
45: Parks Gallery, Taos
2, 50-51: John T. Denne / Shidoni Foundry and Galleries,
Tesuque, New Mexico